Praise for *Local Heroes*

David Tucker celebrates the incandescence of the every day, and raises the ordinary to art—a telephone as quiet as an heirloom, the stillness tended like wheat—even as he mourns the quickness of time passing. There are gems on every page, in every line, in poems full of pathos and humor and longing. And always, the last words linger, still shimmering with a reverence for life amidst all the losses.

—Amy Nutt, Pulitzer Prize winning author

In *Local Heroes* David Tucker, a life-long and award-winning newspaper reporter, delivers hard news while also turning his lyric eye to the hard truth closest at hand: time's forward march. "Daylight Savings Time" opens There is a morning each November/when an hour is given back to us. Yes, we lose it/again in March but for now who cares? Tucker's central concern is that now, rich with mystery and disappointment and wonder. "Talking to the Cat at Four A.M." ends Happiness, I never know/when you're coming/or why. He writes, There will/be glories that never make the newspaper." This wise and mature book is full of such glories.

—Suzanne Cleary. Suzanne Cleary's fourth book of poems, *The Odds*, won the 2004 Laura Boss Narrative Poetry award

David Tucker's new book weaves life in the newsroom, life on the streets, and the failings and flickering joys of his own life in a tenderly honest way. It's telling that the local heroes of his title are women, some of whom live the sorts of lives Thoreau described as quiet desperation, while others, like Aunt Rubena, a county clerk "re-elected fourteen times without opposition" spends her days under" a turret fan that spread a blessing of little breezes/ around the office." To give you an idea of his fine ear, I offer one happiness and one sorrow "a daughter's red sneaker/ sits all afternoon on the windowsill/trying to be quiet" and, of a woman waiting to be taken away, "The boy says why do they call it the crazy house?/ and she said cause they's crazy people in it/I guess, but he doesn't say what he sees now:/ a downpour of words, the rain dogs/running loose out there and life without her."

—Lola Haskins, author of *Homelight* and thirteen other poetry collections

Local Heroes

David Tucker

Regal House Publishing

Contents

Part One 1

Aunt Rubena 3

Loafing 5

Red Peppers. 6

Dear Beth. 7

Little Shoe Napping 8

Angel of a Boring Day 9

Local Heroes 10

Hat of the Moon 11

Daughter Doing Homework at 5 in the Morning 12

The Old Reporter 13

Love in the Kitchen 14

No Pattern the Pattern 15

Driving All Night in the Red States 16

Part Two 17

Monday Song 19

A Muse Walks into a Newsroom 20

Brimstone Sunday 21

Bob's Old Gloves. 22

Rain Dogs 24

My Father Quoting Shakespeare Late at Night. . . 25

At The Emerson Inn. 26

Wonders. 27

The Insomnia Bus Tour 28

Somebody Wake the Verb 29

Obit for Newsprint . . . 30
Wonders No. 2 . . . 31
Miss Sophie . . . 33
Encouragement . . . 35
The House of Old Age . . . 36
Sunday Morning Derelicts . . . 38
Waking to Baseball . . . 40
Whatever, Whatever . . . 42

Part Three . . . 43
Words for Lunch . . . 45
A Fleeting Glimpse . . . 46
Dogwood . . . 47
Talking to the Cat at Four A.M. . . . 48
When I See You Again . . . 50
Morning Meditation During a Hangover . . . 51
In the Clear . . . 53
Self Portrait Using the Word "No" . . . 54
A Priest Named Jet . . . 56
Saturday . . . 57
Two Tornadoes . . . 58
Stakeout . . . 60
The Girl in Chaucer . . . 62
Pearls . . . 63
Canoeing the Buffalo River with Amy . . . 65
After the Divorce . . . 66
Bus to Nowhere . . . 67
Nine O'clock on Knoxville Avenue . . . 68
Wheel Of Fortune Through a Window . . . 69
Lost Together . . . 70
Behind the Walls . . . 71

Saw Dust 72
For Them 73
Daylight Savings Time 74
I Lived in Rags 75
Lithium Days 76
Walking with Joe 78
Nothing for the Morning Paper 79

Acknowledgments 81

Published by
Regal House Publishing, LLC
Raleigh, NC 27605

ISBN -13 (paperback): 9781646036622
ISBN -13 (epub): 9781646036639
Library of Congress Control Number: 2025937278

Cover images and design by © studiochi.art

Printed in the United States of America

Regal House Publishing, LLC
https://regalhousepublishing.com

For my daughters: Calisa, Emily and Amy

Part One

Aunt Rubena

Purple scent from type beaten carbon paper,
everything in triplicate,
the beauty of onion skin documents
corners riffling in the window breeze.
A black Underwood with golden ivy
on the keyboard and gold lettered keys
clattered under her small hands
peanuts floated in a bottle of Dr Pepper, God's drink
on a summer afternoon.

Elected county court clerk 14 times without opposition,
Aunt Rubena, the records woman of Linden, tended
tall red ledgers that went back
through two hundred years of county council sessions,
deeds, and sales, trials and verdicts, the occasional hanging
their pages when opened smelled of fading ink
and old sunshine. Her office is cubicled now,
the perky faces who look up from work stations
wouldn't know about a fiesty woman widowed
at 30 with two kids, doomed to potatoes and poke salad
but saved from that because their mother
could type, read and punctuate in a muddy rivertown
where few could do all three.
From her third floor office you can still see
the red rooftops riding above a cedar tree ocean
and the white firefighter's watchtower miles away
on Hohenwald Ridge. Below the window.
the all-day jabber fest still goes on—old men on benches
the shiftless and lazy, the out of work, farmers
in town for the day going through all the news
about crops and heart surgeries

about the fight at Jabot's Honky Tonk last night,
as they whittle the hot afternoon away.

"Aint they something," Aunt Rubena laughed
calling them her rare topical—not tropical—talking birds.
Then back to work, whispering the words
as they sped across the page.
So much went on here, hard work, commentary
on ignorance, the latest gossip, told with a laugh
you could hear from across the street. Smell of everything
in triplicate like modern blue papyrus
with letter shadows all over it.
Hoofbeat of the keys, judges milling around
in cigar-scented air looking so unhurried.
A turret fan that spread a blessing of little breezes
around the office. a smile that liked the world.
She worked here and never missed a day
for 28 years—you'd be amazed.

Loafing

Will we always be like this—so out of it
we don't notice it's noon until 4 o'clock?

and miss the party we didn't want to attend
anyway. Still in bed curled against each other.

We're lazy, we're hopeless,
We waste our days. We've amounted to nothing.

The things we had to do give up on us, no one
shovels the snow, no one looks at the bank balance.

The cricket that snuck into the kitchen last week,
weeps that it chose to bet on us. Most telling of all:

the dryer in the basement buzzes: "I'm ready"
until it's fed up and goes on alone

wobbling toward night, we're lazy, we're hopeless,
our money jangles and falls through the night .

Red Peppers

Your kiss reminds me

of the red peppers
at the Budapest Cafe,

of a red vinyl raincoat,
one button undone

a splash
of rain getting inside,

the glossy cover
of the child's new book

the juke box that wants
its music played

the first snow in December,
silence everywhere,

So much about to happen.

Dear Beth

Do you remember that old guy
who kept his television going
all night and day in the apartment next door,
remember him? Back in Philadelphia,
when we lived there years ago?
Well, I thought of him today that's all.

How his game shows roared through
the walls, so clear we sometimes
answered the questions as we ate
and the talk show applause
murmuring like distant waves.
There were days I thought he had died—

from a stroke or maybe a fall
and was just lying on the floor
while the television chuckled or cried
and went on selling cars and sleeping pills.
Then we'd hear a faucet or a yawn,
a teaspoon ringing then something like a song.

Retired clerk of some kind I guessed,
salesman, mechanic, dentist or scientist.
We passed him a few times, remember?
As he pulled a shopping cart down the hall
wearing a yellow bow tie, remember him
nodding a smile as he opened his door

and disappeared in the sound of applause.
Well, I thought of him today, that's all.

Little Shoe Napping

On days when nothing happens
a jet loafs overhead, exhaust smoke
gowning behind it.

A paper sack plays in the street,
your overcoat sags
and forgets you.

The wind chases the leaves
and they clatter off the porch
saying, "Hurry!"

On days when nothing happens
the mantle clock calls
the small noises back to the house.

A daughter's red sneaker
sits all afternoon on the windowsill,
trying to be quiet.

Angel of a Boring Day

You were just one day and I'm already
forgetting you, you were dull as Eisenhower
the do-nothing president.
Your sun rose at six, went down at seven
—your weather was clear and mild,
a page of the newspaper lifted its head
around 10 a.m. Whitmanesque sunshine
slouched by the back door
until late afternoon, a hummingbird raided the iris
by the kitchen window and left in an instant of
stolen red. my wife and I were reading by the
fireplace around midnight we didn't even talk
about you, a sort of dignified butler, polite and
unnoticed. Just before we turned out the lights
a random breeze began nudging a pencil off
my desk, a big event in your 24 hours with
us, and that must have been the signal
the silence outside the house was looking
for because in it came and we looked up,
a little sad as the pencil hit the floor
and you got ready to go

Local Heroes

The women of my childhood are still waiting
for life to get better, waiting in beat-up cars
under slow red lights in July, dusty stuffed animals
in the back window animal crackers strewn on
car seats deep circles under red eyes. They are bringing
the sheets from the clothesline after dark,
they are walking to the barn before sunrise.
The milk pail squeaks as it swings from their hands,
but on the return trip it is heavy and silent.
They are dying of hard work and childbearing at 19,
they are waking with a yawn so tired you can hear it
halfway to town; husbands dead and the money gone,
they are tottering from the house trailer ready
for the night shift at the hospital. They are sewing
at dawn, they are mopping while feeding the child
who screams in the high chair and they are feeding
the grandchild in the high chair and the grandfather
on the deathbed, they are working at Pit Stop, Sonic,
the 7-Eleven, bus stations, and Piggly Wiggly,
they are changing bedpans, their names written
on shirt pockets. They are shelling peas under
the oak—it's 99 degrees in the shade, they
are churning butter in the breezeway—
sweat rills their foreheads. They are waiting in rattling cars
under slow red lights, rubbing their eyes,
pressing fingers down on that ache
on the bridge of the nose, taking a deep breath
as the light over the road goes green.

Hat of the Moon

That the apple tree bloomed overnight,
the mild white flowers
suddenly just there when I woke
and that apple scent,
thin and calm, that lingers two weeks then gone.
That my wife rummaged her jewelry box
for the day's ear rings, a towel wrapped
around her, that lovemaking as we glanced
at the clock radio, late for work
our breaths held in a cry. That quiet in the newsroom
when I got there, lasting only a few minutes
a reporter standing at my office door news to tell,
gradually irritated that I wasn't listening.
That glass of ice tea sweating on a window sill
as early deadlines arrived like a swarm of bees
and the silence that took over
an hour later on one side of the room,
spreading out slowly to every desk,
what the stories said, that list of things that
had to be done and the none of them that
got done, the drive home,
the commuter train's reflection coasting
beside it down the river, that moon
strolling past the cafes and the boathouses
on the embankment, tossing its battered
hat softly into the sky.

Daughter Doing Homework at 5 in the Morning

I woke to the rustle of cornflakes down in the kitchen
The thump of the refrigerator door, rattle of a chair
dragged across the floor. Who could be up
so early, only a ray of sunlight in the trees
And the house still dark and cold?

But I knew it had to be you, my intense,
passionate child. And came downstairs to find you
digging your cereal bowl from the cupboard,
lugging the milk and the orange juice
to the table. I watched as you sat down
and spread blank paper in front of you
as if you had serious work to do
before first-grade class began later in the day.

Holding your pencil in that painful,
crooked grip, you began to count in whispers,
stopping now and then for a bite of cereal.
Then you looked up and saw me, "Hi, Daddy."
You have homework, I asked. "Yes. lots," you said.

I wanted to take you in my arms,
but you were busy with important work to do,
so I made coffee, washed the dishes
brought you another glass of juice,
did anything I could think of to stay close
to the concentration on your face
at five o'clock in the morning.

The Old Reporter

The young reporters are
taking bets on when she'll
croak and whether
it will happen in the
newsroom or the bar next
door. Her cough has
already wounded the roses
the staff gave her for her
birthday. Her hands tremble
at the keyboard and she
forgets which story
she told you last—living on cigarettes
and vodka and the fights she can pick.
The publisher is offering her
retirement, a buyout, a party,
a plaque. It's that, or life
on the obit desk. She can't
hold out much longer, our
good ol' girl, who was quick
and brassy and saw
through shit in the wild,
early days of LBJ.

Love in the Kitchen

Pretty woman,
slicing the green pepper
with moody glances,

let me kiss
that elegant neck.

Delicious woman you
with the blinding ass.

Hours of talk like this,
days of gross pleading
until my knees were numb,
my groin a bruised stone.

Then, in the late evening
At the end of a century
she turned to me,

laughing and slowly
lifting her dress.

No Pattern the Pattern

A car sped through last night's dream
 a newspaper did an airy cartwheel,

a derelict on a bench sat up and
yawned in a town I've never seen.

Some things never get stitched together
sometimes no pattern is the pattern.

Someone stepped into the road and tossed
a pan of water upon the snow

and with the same motion flung
the stars out though the winter trees.

Disconnected actions were revered
in that city, that and stillness tended like wheat.

No pattern the pattern. And as for the storms
that spun through in the spring,

what can you do about the weather?
Or the shadows walking quiet streets

carrying brooms to sweep the snow away.
And I never did guess who that stranger was

in the Panama hat, who came out of a house
at dawn, walked to the front gate

and looked down the road a long
time for something not here yet.

Driving All Night in the Red States

I will drive all night in the Red States
I will take the back roads through illiterate towns,
with one redlight, I will shop Walmarts
that stay open late, their windows
festooned with assault rifles and Wonder Bread
at discounts that will make me weep.

I will make my peace with Jesus billboards
that glow from hilltops and welcome signs decorated
with bullet holes,
I will accept
the confusion of flag-emblazoned pickups,
the twinkle of their gun racks. And give in
to the longing of satellite dishes as they turn
to early bird jewelry sales at four in the morning.

I will marry the trailer park beauty
who sits in a lawn chair beside a road, winding
pink curlers into her hair, I will slouch
in a lawn chair beside her, smoking Camels
as the sun comes up. I will reject national healthcare

and muslims, I will ban homos and burn newpapers,
I will denounce foreign nations, ambitious women
and abortion, I will oppose foodstamps and Spanish,
I will wave to everyone who passes,
glad to see them, glad to see them go.

Part Two

Monday Song

For this was Monday, a plain old day.
There was a lot of leaning back
to be done, a lot of looking out windows,
a black cat slept in her favorite chair
a breeze twirled a dusty wing

in a cobweb. This was Monday, seen from
a study on a hill it dreamed up the first page
of a novel, possibilities for how
a world history might begin as nothing
but weather and spare accounts

of light and silence.
This was Monday bland and even the telephone
was quiet as an heirloom. A wet leaf clung
to a window, scratched and dark
like an old Elvis record.

and the snow hurried down the sidewalk
chasing the late postman. An hour later
I rode an elevator to the newsroom
while back home my cat opened a yellow eye
on Monday, a plain old day.

A Muse Walks into a Newsroom

What are you doing here
in the newsroom at three in the afternoon,
in Newark, New Jersey of all places
looking so pretty despite those
(And are those really) blood-red fingernails
and is that a missing tooth.
As you stroll from outta nowhere
down the aisles between
the workstations and glide past
the reporters who are bent almost
double like bike racers, typing
too fast to even look up
your heels lightly clicking
as if timed to the clatter
of some other keyboard.
Are you the spirit of breaking news,
our homicide muse?
a lovely scandal not yet discovered
but close now very close
who are you really, making
me forget
my life like this?

Brimstone Sunday

Thunder is gentler than Brother Harve
when he gets warmed up in that church by the river.
Souls are sore from a week of farming, lust
is rising and everyone is all jammed
together, aftershave and slicked back hair,
the women bright and edible in their
flowery hats with their big cleavage showing.
Break out the cardboard fans, my brother,
the ones with Jesus on the front,
nailed up like a water drop.
It's hot and will soon get hotter.
And here he comes striding to the pulpit, tall
and fanatic thin, his white hair sticking out in
electric wisps as he begins, hitting the air and
saying his favorite sermon words:
"And God Smote Them!"
And we all jump—as awake as breaking
glass! "We are not worthy," he hollers,
"Not worthy of God's Love!"
And *wham!* goes his fist because our sins demand it.
And he staggers around weeping about
the grace of God so lost on us.
Women cry. Men stare
at their hands, saying Amen.
What a mess.
When it's over there will be dinner
on the ground, fried chicken, baked
beans and iced tea in big jars
under the trees.
But we have to go through this
to get to that.

Bob's Old Gloves

What would he say to see me
shoveling snow from the drive
this morning wearing his old gloves?

My guess: "Hey, those are great gloves
aren't they? Glad their yours now."
Then he'd chatter about where he
bought them the price, the many reasons
leather gloves are the best. "At K-Mart
you can always get really good deals on
gloves and other things."

He was always putting people at ease
finding small talk in the most boring
details. Even near the end.
"Hey, those are some nice shoes,"
he'd say. Remember to polish the
backs of the heels,
So they shine when you turn to leave a room or say
goodbye, making a good last impression.

The sky is blue and the snow light
as thought as I shovel steadily down the driveway.
I could keep going like this for hours,

pausing now and then to pull Bob's gloves on tight
and hear him say, "I guess you're goanna
be here for a while,"
as he goes inside the house
to watch football, then turns

"got those at K-Mart, years ago."
Later, Bob, I say, the way
he'd want me to say it
casual, without looking up.

Rain Dogs

She says raising you kids is just the same
as beating my head against a wall
and the boy thinks: *well, fine, don't hurt yourself.*
Her bruises may be imaginary, but they make
the air smell new like that paint smell
after lightning. She's about to go to the asylum
the next day, third trip, so what can she say
about anything anyway? Now she asks:
Don't the rain remind you of chickens
pecking the window trying to get at us?
He thinks about it:—*No,* he says, *but I do see*
an angel scrawling a name on glass.
How 'bout that?
*W*hoa, she says, then you should be going, too.
They watch the long corn rows bend down,
the trees tip back on their heels, she shivers,
whoa, this rain looks like Baboon Daddy with a mad on,
throw those gobs of leaves into the air, you fool, fooly old fool
she cheers, drag your hairy
cloud self over the road to town.
tomorrow I go, she says, then skips over
the whole thing asking—this window isn't it like a movie?
The towns folks running through hail, their coats
flopping over their heads.
The boy says *why do they call it the crazy house?*
and she says cause they's crazy people in it,
"I guess," but he doesn't say what he sees now:
a downpour of words, the rain dogs
running loose out there and life without her.

My Father Quoting Shakespeare Late at Night

Other fathers may also have lived a work
in progress entitled: "I Blame the World for Everything,"
that began soon after dinner, but how many
were also bent on reciting every line of Shakespeare
learned in high school? "Let "me have about me
"bald, slick-headed men such as sleep at night.
"Yon Cassius," he strides across the cracked linoleum of
that drafty house, trying to remember the rest,
"has a lean and hungry look." Dutifully seated
on the couch with the cigarette holes
in the vinyl arms, my brothers and I glance
at each other. One of us must be Cassius-like,
with Cassius thoughts so obvious. Then came
"the sea of trouble" as he crumpled
his bank statement in his fist and added
his own troubles to the sea, "Do you know
what the bank can do with this?" We knew.
Miles away, a semi-truck began the long
climb up highway 100 toward Nashville.
Crickets sang out by the fence, safe
from anger and Shakespeare. There was a faint
grin on my father's face,
so pleased he was to remember golden
lines in those hard days: "The quality of
"mercy is not strained it falleth
"like a gentle rain…" as he turned for bed
and made a slight bow to the crowd.

At The Emerson Inn

Quarreling with her about nothing
sent me into these doldrums—that should not
have been unexpected after she left (Taking her book,
her thoughts, her eyes, her moods—like weather—
and going to the beach.)

What are the chances she will
just come back and say sorry?
Well, none.
Yeah, I'm betting none.

I'll stay in this room and stare
at the Bonsai Garden on the lovely
antique writing desk while the afternoon
shadows move in interesting ways
over the perfect little trees and the jade guy
with a pleasant smile fishes
his life away from a matchstick bridge,
though there is nothing to be caught
in the clear shining pool.

Evening arrives and
the penetrating scent of suntan oil
as she enters the room glistening,
then taps me on the shoulder
and asks: "Are you awake?"

Looking out from the third-floor window,
I could see there was a world outside
Clapboard bungalows on leafy streets, vacationers
talking on porches, radios playing and kids
on their bikes, racing past.

Wonders

The morning goes too fast to be clearly seen.
Something breaks in the kitchen,
a cat slinks up the stairs.

There will be evidence everywhere, spoons
and spent cereal bowls on the floor
licked bright—no one will confess.

A daughter will giggle as she scampers
down the street to the bus, book bag bouncing
on her back. I will tie my shoes

as the snow begins. I'll look for my wallet
as the minutes go by, I will not remember where
I left my keys, only that this is another morning

lived too fast. The daughter's radio
will be playing a light song in a distant room
left on for the day.

"Am I the only one dizzy from the events
of the last three minutes," I will ask
the duplicitous cat and she will blink

her slow yellow eyes as the bathroom door
opens, as a naked woman
with a towel on her head runs past.

The Insomnia Bus Tour

On the insomnia bus tour again
circling the brightly lit town

I know all the stops by now
recognize the regulars.

We ride slowly along and don't speak.
Soon, our guide will hand out tickets

To the zombie musical. Seen it,
seen it, seen it a hundred times.

Drunks are staggering to the street.
No, not drunk, just sleepy.

Around sunrise, a few dreams finally begin their house calls,

a noiseless snow starts filling
tire tracks and foot prints.

putting everything back
the way it was.

Somebody Wake the Verb

We arrived at the wake for our old teacher
Mr. John Lorili Randolph the Third, after his long
but graceful death. It was a modest and sad affair,
well attended by students from long ago, by poets, colleagues,
city officials and by the parts of speech that mingled among
us trying to look human. I saw you, Blue Article, peeking
between the wreaths of roses—sobbing "a's" and "the's."
Now listen, Adjective, you can't keep saying
the great, wondrous, brilliant man and think
people won't just stop listening. Prepositions,
you drank too much again, before, during and after it all.
We signed the book, listened more polite than
mournful as the speeches went on and on. Some
remembered the day he turned us
into words and demanded we arrange ourselves
into sentences, and his heretical stance
against the comma, "Take them all out," he shouted.
And weeks later, "Now put a few back in."
and his requirement that we be ready
to recite a poem instantly and without warning.
As the wake continued, late sunlight paused
over the noble face of the noun. "There
"must be a memorial service," he said,
"so that the nouns may speak." It was good
to see classmates from way back, though we felt
a bit lost without our hero. But no one
was going anywhere anyway—
not while the beautiful verb slept it off
in the next room, still in her ball gown
and her pearls, so late the next day.

Obit for Newsprint

Mayors were beautiful when they
were led off to jail their hands
cuffed before them on mornings
that started out so dull
but the newspapers are closing,
The Aurora, the *Bulletin,* the *Mirror*, the *Sun*
who will put the new mayor in jail?

Ex-presidents were lovely
and considerate to die on slow news days
and we thank the governor
who gave jobs to his lovers, cops on the take,
the wife who sawed her husband into parts
on a sunny Tuesday
The Citizen, the *Eagle,* the *Gazette* and *The Press*
Who will let the facts have their day?

When a hurricane drives the
ocean mad and it pours across
Water Gap bridge and the
townsfolk pile up sandbags and
the priest shovels sand
The Oracle, the *Beacon, Mercury* and the *Star*

beside the convicts let out for
the night in their orange
jumpsuits! who will ask
how the dam broke, who built it,
and from what?
Where all the money went?
Not the *Messenger*, or the *Scimitar*, not the *Press* or *Tribune.*

Wonders No. 2

I was driving down my usual road
on my way to work this morning
when I had to slam on my brakes
to let a Canadian goose
limp onto the pavement to get to City Lake.
Black head held high
bobbing forward a little
it kept eyes straight ahead
and touched the blacktop
lightly—on an injured leg
just enough to maintain
a listing balance,
as it reached the grass embankment
then slipped into the water
bugling triumph
amid a ruckus of car horns.

Seconds later, a little further down
the same road just before my turn
a man I've seen many times
straggled down the sidewalk to the corner store
lifting a forearm up ahead of him
with each left-foot step
to lighten some of his weight
just enough to keep the pressure off
a twisted foot that came down
sideways as he focused
on what was ahead of him
awkward yet graceful for what it was
getting just a little quicker
as he neared the store

eventually almost skipping along.
All day at work I kept remembering
what Jesus said about our ordinary days:
"Except ye see signs and wonders"
"you will in no wise believe."

Miss Sophie

In that dilapidated schoolroom
where the Santa Claus we crayoned last year
is peeling off the door, where the first day
of spring it's hard to do anything but
think of sneaking off to the river
first chance we get, be quiet please!
Miss Sophie is talking up there at
the front of the room about the dreaded
subject we will never master: Cursive Writing.
The thing that separates winners
from losers. "Oh, foolish ones," she is
saying as she walks the desk rows,
ruler in her hand, a round woman
with a bad temper and a faith in
disappointment: "Don't think to get
by in this life with just printing out
the letters. People will soon decide
you're just some ignorant hillbilly
and they will be right, that's all you'll be."

And she says this with, I think,
way too much gusto, daring us to
break from rural generations of
failure, taunting us with the prospect
of a future of field work, welfare, moonshine,
10 dirty kids and a rusty Ford on
blocks in the front yard.
Cursed by a spell of ignorant sentences.
There is a row of apples on her desk.
they gleam like no other apples, shined
ruby-red on the dresses of the

teacher's pets. The boy
at the desk in front of me, who gets
beaten by Miss Sophie every day, is
asleep on his arm. Beside me, a girl
with pony-tail hair, writes in flowing
script even as Miss Sophie lectures
about it. The letters curve and loop
together, hooks and beaks joined in
a dance of blue ink—and she sighs as she inspects
each word and looks up at teacher's smile.

My own script book is splotched with stick
letters stumbling into each
other like passengers in a train
wreck. But it's a breezy day in
early spring; blackbirds race past
the schoolroom door
Thunderheads sail along the river.
Even Miss Sophie stops her lecture to stare,
making the beauty official and allowing
this moment of escape to linger. It's a
long time until three o'clock, forever
until the clouds move away, eternity
until the report cards come with
grades that will show we'll all
be hillbillies one day soon.

ENCOURAGEMENT

From the cat who jumps on the desk
purring like a sonnet; from the honest spider
knitting her treatise on Kant, spreading it out
in the stalks of the white begonia.
from the bravery of the comely moth
that walks the lip of the red flowerpot
like Danger Girl, like tipsy John Berryman,
help from things that just come and go.
From wind that wanders the shining bamboo
as if about to speak and from the newspaper
on the table that lifts its big wings in welcome
and from the student reading by a window,
she and her book silent, neither of them really there
and a yawn declaring its relief in a distant room.
From the smell of cut grass
that hauls its veil through the afternoon,
the peacefulness of it and from the crow
who lives nearby as she floats
over the house, coming and going
as she pleases on black shining wings,
from the inertia of the Ford on concrete blocks, weeds rising
into the engine, from the backyard dog who always
finds a happy fight to roll in.

The House of Old Age

The turning of the pages of a magazine
in the middle of a morning sends
waiting room echoes through the quiet
house echoes that are making us old.

The routines that hold us closer to them
and this sense that steady notice is
being taken of us somewhere now, this
is making us old and the objects with
us for so many years
the way they watch the changes to
our skin and voices, listening for
repeated stories, the books that eye
us and glance sidelong at each other,
the yawns declaring themselves
a little louder and coffee being poured,
sounding harsher because the house
is quieter by degrees,
all this makes us old.

And the weather that has been light
and blue for weeks is also making us
old. Years of love have made us old,
lovemaking in all our different beds
and houses, the painstaking care
of children, sleepless nights,
work and promises have made
us old. I touch your hand in
the night, your sleeping face,
and we still make promises about the
future but smile about what we can't stop.

Thin clouds skim across the moon.
Nights are cool with a little wind.
We leave the windows
open and more old age
comes in.

Sunday Morning Derelicts

They come straggling down Broad
Street crawling out of the
underpasses at dawn staggering
from cardboard boxes, moving
like shivering scraps of paper.

They scuttle through the city hall
courtyard, creeping out of alley ways,
they glide like thin smoke, vanish around
a corner, a shoulder peeking back at you.

One goes panhandling under the morning moon
in a long shining coat of garbage bags
and garbage bag shoes,
another pounds his fist
at the air as you pass. Maybe

they had parents once
mothers, maybe sisters and brothers, now
voices fly at them like bats and visions
ride around and through them on
broomsticks, though gray and grimy
jailhouse weather.

Here is one who calls herself
"Pharoah" pharoah, pharoah, cairo,
gizmo," barefoot, ragged and slow,
listing to one side as her breath fogs away.

And here is another, swaggering
along the waterfront streets.

Tipping a moth-eaten fedora, blowing
smoke rings. You ask who he is,
who he was as he goes.

Waking to Baseball

Waking at two in the morning
with the radio still playing
and the announcers wrapping up
the Yankee's game from California
is like waking in the back row
of a seminar where old scholars debate
the same questions every night
as decades pass. Next week, next year,
they will still be talking about slumps
that arrive from nowhere and stay
for reasons never known. How can you
see which slump is real, they ask
once again, until it emerges day
by day and numbers eventually confirm
the relentless dismay? And of tonight's game,
what dare we conclude?
There is no denying the Yankees blew a lead

in the eighth. But the play of the new right
fielder gives hope and so does
the relief work of the southpaw
just called up from Columbus.
And yet, these are vague implications, what
can we deduce with so few facts before us
in May when each increment of the
season carries import not clear until October?
Through the radio, I can hear stadium crews
Vacuuming the aisles in Anaheim, brooms clacking
against wooden seats, someone hollering
across the grandstands as the announcers
read the last scores from the National League.

A thin smell of dogwood enters the room
here in New Jersey as I yawn and go back
to sleep. A long season. One loss, light as
my blanket, means nothing yet

Whatever, Whatever

When you reach 55, you get
up with the birds at 5 o'clock
to take a piss, look up a line in a
book, check out the moonlight—
whatever.

Fog leans its ghost face
through the trees, saying let
me guess
the time left for you.
Names and phone numbers emerge

from a blue haze on the horizon.
You're not sure you've seen them before.
But you've learned from your kids to say
whatever—because it just means
—whatever.

The blue jay's song, earthy and sharp
says: pay attention, old fart,
here you are; the morning has a date,
and you are in it, this is
your place.

Who has time for such trivia,
you say, continuing to turn away
to your very important other business
the whatever of whatever.

Part Three

Words for Lunch

I went down to the K-mart in West Orange avoiding the news-
room, letting lunch hour go another hour on a Friday afternoon.
Business was slow, K-Mart a museum of itself
with everything on sale. Three or four bargain hunters
wandered the aisles unhurried, considering the ninety-nine
dollar suits touching the arms of fall jackets
hung in rows of moody browns and blues. Clerks read
newspapers and talked in a listless hum, offering solutions

to the government shutdown while leaning
across counters and someone wondered what good
is the death penalty? Shirts labeled "Clearance" whispered
"jail the immigrants." Cheap jewelry shined in the after-
noon sun, saying there is still time to buy something

that will change your life.
in a dirt-shined suit chewed a chocolate donut
and sipped black coffee, looking past the parking lot, care-
fully considering his choice for the Supreme Court.

A few more shoppers were getting out of their cars,
a child straggled along from a hand.
And the woman who ran that little dining section
that tended a wheel of hotdogs that sweated
in the baking light. I didn't want to go back
to the newspaper. The bluelight specials
had just begun and Marvin Gaye was singing
on the music spool, singing his heart out.

A Fleeting Glimpse

Driving home from Tennessee one night a few years ago
maybe it was several years ago, I was flooring it past
those little towns with one red light and a gas station
until I came to a baseball game lit up
on the edge of one of those towns but maybe
it wasn't a small town really. Might have been Akron,
it might have been. It was late, maybe it was midnight,
the game gone into extra innings, but I don't know that.
I was speeding by and I'm surprised any of the memory
is left. Only a few spectators were still in the stands
parents probably, seen from the road
twin vases side by side on a shelf—that's how I see them now.
The radio said the stock market was depressed,
And there would be war, a news reader mumbled
like an elf hiding under a bed, well, they all
sound that way to me and there's always a war
about to end or about to begin.
The infielders were likely crouched,
hands and gloves on knees. I think the players
were all kids, older kids, maybe high schoolers.
A blue halo surrounded the light stanchions
and the early dew shimmered on the outfield grass,
but if don't recollect that for sure, it's still safe
to say it did. The pitcher nodded to the catcher—
well, they do that, don't they—and wheeled into motion,
leg kick, arm-whirl, a white blur from the slingshot
of a right hand, coulda been left. I never knew what
happened next since I had to keep going,
to reach Michigan by morning or some other place.
But in my daydreams, I've often stopped and parked
to watch the game, go on and on into the morning,
what I remember of it and what I don't.

Dogwood

And the dogwood that almost died a few times that had so
much contention,

marooned in the rocky part of the back yard cramped between
a bullying oak
and a light-and-rain-eating pine,

limbs broken and re-broken, scarred by an ice storm
bruised by a grandson's baseball bat

has spread ragged branches
out into an awkwardly tilted green and white umbrella again this
spring, a wisp

from a Chinese watercolor, flattened
to elegance, leaning too far out for balance,
in the June morning yet balanced anyway.

Talking to the Cat at Four A.M.

I fell asleep reading
in the late afternoon

and woke in the dark
years behind
in all I had to do.

Where was I,
what had I
missed? Where

was I supposed to
be? But gradually I saw

that this was my house,
my neighborhood, my town.

And really, what
did I have to do?
Nothing.

And where was I
supposed to be?
Nowhere.

So, nothing
And nowhere called to me as
I made coffee

and took my time. Rain
wandered down

the leaves by the window.

My cat jumped onto
my lap It was four
in the morning.

Happiness, I never know
when you're coming
or why.

When I See You Again

I lie where you lay
and breathe the smell of you
on the pillow

the grey street light
slants through the
blinds light rain
spatters the sill

You are gone
until I don't
know when

Morning Meditation During a Hangover

It was an amazing morning
for one so slow to wake, so clumsy
at pouring coffee, so good at spilling it, so forgetful
of what he did the night before, what
he said, where he visited, what
he dreamed about, so unsteady,
so unwilling to speak
as his family slid by like fish,
wife and children turning their heads
to gaze in slow motion at the half intelligible
specter that was him. Just sitting down
on the couch, in his favorite corner of it,
took a day off his life and with great effort
he waited to see what his first
lucid thought might be.
"Fall," something said, offering
evidence in a delicate procession
of jolts that proved the sky
was clear and harsh like a mad monk's whip.
Leaves rattled with a yellow letting go
and that low autumn light was arranging
gothic shadows of branches on the Chinese carpet.
A radio said "October 29th." Said it with total
confidence, making him think
he might be alive, reviving
the one dubious faith that still, sometimes,
seemed to work for him—the faith
that sooner or later his troubles
would bore him and they were in fact

starting to do that now which made it
a rather amazing morning, considering that he was
actually going to be OK, maybe.

In the Clear

for Steve Lopez

One morning in April or maybe October,
I'll be in the clear. Whatever I have
Of love, work or money will be enough.
It'll be like a happy wake, but it won't be that.
It'll be like a party but it won't be that either.
I'll just be in the clear.
The DMV kept a file on me but it disappeared.
There's a warrant out there with my name on it
But it's fallen behind the sheriff's desk.
A disease is coming but its been delayed, mishaps sped by and
missed me, making no sound.

Whatever it is I'll probably escape
the next thing coming or maybe not
either way. I'll be in the clear someday.

Self Portrait Using the Word "No"

No more television.
No more television?
No more television,
You have screwed around all day long
neglected your family, your writing, your chores, sprawled
on the couch like a fish on the sea bottom.
And no more McDonalds either.

No more McDonalds?
No more McDonalds, you're getting fat,
your heart hums in the morning from the junk you eat.

and no more staying up late.
I love staying up late,
I'm afraid I will miss something.

No staying up late, it's bad for you, you wake up like a crazed cyclone barely making it to work, nerves pounding temper flaring, cursing your job.
Staying up late is out.

Who's talking to me?

Someone.

I don't like you, someone.
And while we are at it, no more Jack Daniels.

No way I give that up.
I love the clatter of ice cubes

In those heavy glasses. That's all
No more Jack. You don't know how to just have a social drink,
you drink to get drunk,
you're already borderline alcoholic. No more Jack.
But all these things make me happy.

No more being happy.
Look what it does to you.

A Priest Named Jet

On television tonight they
recreated the mumification
of a priest named Jet
a middle-aged Theban two thousand years dead.

Tenderly did the priests embalm ol' Jet
and gently with linen did they fill
his head storing brain and heart in a
golden vase.

May the rest of my days be soft,
may all my worries be removed
from my head and all
my hereafters be linen like Jet's

SATURDAY

Saturday, stay light and blue

like this—be a masterpiece
of a day paint
the wildflowers venetian red

radiate a vermillion breeze, ochre a
yellow bumble bee that bumps against
the ceiling.

Saturday, set up your easel, get out
your ragged straw hat,
paint the lightness of Saturday.

Two Tornadoes

Two tornadoes hit my hometown, only one
was weather, a snake of a wind that killed three,
the other is still rampaging, fed
by painkillers, alcohol, Valium, Xanex,
coke, speed, sleeping pills, OxyContin, and
Meth. Look out for afternoons that end early,
for purple night blowsing, for low clouds
bending trees to the ground, then a green quiet
that won't last long. Some people notice—
when it's too late—that the air is suddenly
an upside down Christmas tree, spinning cars
and mobile homes around itself for decoration,
windows shake, doors fly open, chairs become
gymnasts, the sunset is faint red
like a beat-up clown face and the satellite dishes
lift away in unison at the Merry Meadows Trailer Park.
Good-bye Piggly Wiggly, meth labs explode
in the woods, farewell to Wal-Mart—Wal-Mart, you're gone.
A young man blows his leg off so he can live on
prescription drugs, another hangs himself, saying he was
bored, and another drives off a bridge waving
good-bye as he goes. The drug-addicted drug counselor
writes his novel in a halfway house,
the real estate agent quotes Jung as he sells you land
not for sale, the religious bulldozer driver quotes
the Bible while punching holes in the wall, zombies
line up at midnight begging for pills at the hospital
emergency room, nerves curled up like apple peels.
Old people sleep in snowy medication valleys;
left home to care for themselves,
they finally strike out on their own and disappear

into the funneling air. Two tornados, mad as Hell,
wide as a judgment, twisting souls into licorice
as they float up to the sky, stay gone awhile,
then come falling back down through
the exposed plumbing and the trees.

STAKEOUT

I really don't mind staking
out the house where
the murder suspect lives.
I only need

a few quotes. Well, maybe just
one. I just want five minutes.
Ok, Ok, maybe one minute
of your valuable time,
Sir.

But nothing is
moving inside.
It's hard to see when
all the lights in the house are off.

A pickup parked
in the gravel driveway
seems to be making a face
at me and I don't feel good

about the Confederate flag
on the back window
or the gun rack. Which
is empty.

It has rained all
morning and now
I'm drowsy
from the metronome patter.

If he is inside the house,
he could be watching me
as I take notes on him.
I guess I will have to walk
up to the front steps and knock.

Or I could just go
back to the newsroom: and say
no one answered the door
and technically speaking that
would be true.

The Girl in Chaucer

The teacher swept in holding books
against his chest, squinting through thick glasses,
a gaze that said: "Is this where I'm supposed to be?"
And the students looked up like fish.
I made my way to the back of the room,
to a chair beside a woman with long dark hair,
wan, elegant face—and was that a smile?
Soon I would find out that she was
from Ohio by way of England and lately Boston
by way of Detroit by way of a boyfriend
half-ditched that I would soon wish drafted or dead.
I would find out she played piano,
liked the Detroit Tigers, had a small scar
on her knee, that she signed up for this class
at the last minute. Her hands guided the words
as she talked and all the while her breasts
there, with soft definition there under
a black wool sweater.
Oh yeah, and she'd just
arrived in town,
on the 7:30 train from Boston.

Pearls

As I read this lovely book of poems,
holed up in my office late on a rainy night
in a newsroom at the end of the world,
Yang Wan Li is chanting for a little while
in a 12th-century village where rain falls
"like pearls spilling onto a glass plate."

But I'm here in Newark, New Jersey
having an almost nervous breakdown:
there are no stories for tomorrow's paper
and the reporter who almost has a scoop for page one
has not called. So, we're just about fucked.

But part of me must like it here
just the slightest worrying part
the part that is never happy—the part that doubts
the politicians, the cops, the neighbor,
the Salavation Army, the weather, the time the sun sets.
That part seems to like it here.

The newsroom is almost beautiful,
I will allow that is true
if a sort of relentless tension can be beautiful
if carjackings are beautiful and the scandals
that grow like mushrooms from the mayor's fingers.

A few voices mutter on the other side
of the room, as if some basic elemental
rhythm has taken over and has been revealed
as nothing more than the scattered pecking
of spirits on keyboards .

I say almost a lot, almost happy
almost in love, almost taking too many drugs
almost too old to do this anymore.

Part of me must like being almost in two places at once
In the village where Yang wakes
as rain falls and as he gives in to old age
saying at last he understands the rain
and here in a newsroom in a drizzling city,
at the end of the world, where silhouettes
holding umbrellas move in a faceless waltz

and gather at the corner to fix
the bid for the next bridge contract.

Some part of me must like this almost suspended
slightly concerned, spooky. almost pleasant mood
must like waiting to see whether the reporter
with tomorrow's story has jumped to another paper,
run off with the night clerk, quit without notice
or is driving like mad to get here
through rain that is falling like pearls.

Canoeing the Buffalo River with Amy

For a long time we did nothing but coast
down that fine old happy river, past farms
that failed years ago, fences toppling
under honeysuckle. We meandered
past the nursing home and the patients
lined up in rockers, waving, but soon
we were bumping from one bank to the other,
ducking the green overhang as the river buckled
and the canoe shot through the narrows,
juddered and shook in the shoals at Bethel Bluff,
spun backwards, almost tipping over.
Our yells echoed off the sheer slate walls,
scraggy cedars growing out of the rock,
looked down, black in the sun glare.
Near Flatwoods, the water was still and blue
turtles slept in trees, blinking droopy eyes,
the whole afternoon to waste.
Lets never get in a hurry again, we said,
like drunks taking the pledge, but for this day
we meant it. Then a mile of silence and horseflies,
scent of cornbread from an unseen house,
voices up ahead and dock lamps shining
through the trees, still far away.

After the Divorce

With the curried chicken bubbling in a skillet
and steam running down the windows,
I kissed this woman I met only an hour ago
touched her palm with my tongue and tasted
that bit of red pepper there. You know,
there is this rainy street in Budapest
and I'm fairly sure of it, with a misty cafe,
though I've never seen it, and a sign
that spells OPEN with a flickering O
and a curry good for what ails you.

Bus to Nowhere

The bus idles in a town we've never seen.
We get off to look around but there's no one in
the dark station house, an old sign groans
vaguely in the wind.

A crowd was here a while ago
caroling under the dark pavilions.
Footprints lead away
in different directions over the snow,

voices are fading into the fields.
What town is this, we ask.
The driver waves his slow all aboard. By now
we know he never answers

that the trip lasts as long as it lasts.
Exhaust smoke floats into the clear night,
the bus is heavily calm like the distance
behind it, before it.

Nine O'clock on Knoxville Avenue

It's nine o-clock on my old street.
The children are getting spanked
into their beds, televisions light
the rooms with blue gunfire
and somewhere up the block, a man
and a woman argue about something unintelligible.
He shouts as if about to hit her, she screams
as if she can't take their life anymore
and can't leave it either.
"Just get the fuck away from me," she hollers.
Their anger wanders from room to room
strengthening, subsiding. His bellow
follows her down a hallway and every
few paces she turns and yells, "You bastard!"
Then someone throws a plate against a wall.
Out on the stoop, drinking beer, smoking
and talking, we stop and look toward
the silence, trying to guess
which house is fighting tonight.

Wheel Of Fortune Through a Window

There was a half moon
over the neighborhood,
the biggest I can remember, pale
blue seas just above the treeline.
There was a cough somewhere
down the street, laughter
from late swimmers trudging
in from the beach. A newsless day
a nothing evening.
As I walked back to my house
three of my neighbors, all past 80,
were watching *Wheel of Fortune* together
same routine every weeknight.
Sal and George and Mary.
I could read the questions
from the sidewalk, see the three
of them leaning in
shoulders touching, wheel spinning.

Lost Together

We were talking so much we missed
our turn for the interstate and wandered
onto a road overgrown with sage grass
near an abandoned farm in Kentucky

The hills were getting dark as we sat
on the hood of the car and drank coffee
from a thermos. Bullfrogs choired up
saying they so seldom have visitors

swallows careened through the barn loft.
The farm was peaceful as a ghost ship
passing through ready to move on
in the morning of a century later.

We stayed there for about an hour
talking about what I don't remember
then found our way back to 1-95
and on to Detroit by morning.

Years later,
I remember the pleasure of being with you
that night in no hurry
lost for a while in Kentucky

Behind the Walls

Carpenters left their sandwich wrappers
between the walls, calculations
of the depth of windowsills
are still here, figured in pencil
under the gold wall paper
And the woman who lived here 30 years
left paintings in the attic,
pastel orchids from summer days
and paintings of giant fish,
yellow and green with hard
blood-red fins along their backs.

She died of brain tumor, her husband said,
the day we took the keys to the house.
He stood in the yard talking about her
tears in his eyes.
"She became a little unbalanced,
near the end " he said, "Well, a lot on some days."
But she kept on painting, he said,
and the fish grew large and bright.

Saw Dust

A power saw grinds away
somewhere in the woods

"I'm doing this", it growls,
"doing this all day long."

Son of Hobbes, single-minded
with no doubts—

keep on grinding even
as snow scatters down.

The uneventful hours
walk through my study

through my body
and out the window.

I've been so lazy what
will I do the rest of the day?

Let the scent of sawdust
come to me. let the saw eat

the night and moon
praising the hard life,

amid other sounds vaguely
heard or not heard at all

and things glimpsed or not
glimpsed at all.

For Them

bill collectors gathering at their names,
who keep the television on all day,
shades pulled; their rooms lit by soap operas
and talk show applause, for them.
no culture but Hank Williams and Bob Dylan and AA meetings
car broken down in the front yard and leaking
oil onto the grass and no money to fix it, for them.
Living where the dust jumps from corners
and the fridge is so dirty the Marines couldn't clean it, for them,
living in houses where cats sleep on the kitchen table,
in sagging clapboard neighborhoods where curses rebound
through the alleyways and down the long night road, for them.
sitting in all-night diners, drinking their endless cups of coffee,
for them.
Who smell like tobacco, who think McDonald's is some kind
of spa,
who ride the bus all day going nowhere, who make a pocket
of routine, invisible in our midst, who find
a crack to slip through, who hide in open daylight,
for them, for those just hanging on.

Daylight Savings Time

There is a morning each November
When an hour is given back to us. Yes, we lose it
again in March but for now who cares?

For now we live the grasshopper life.
Rain may be headed our way
this afternoon, or so the radio says,

but there will be snow tomorrow
lovely snow falling in the later dark. There will
be glories that never make the paper.

Death will forget to set his watch
Arriving an hour early and told to wait outside.
Morning sex will last so long dinosaurs

will have time to evolve into birds,
the loud muffler on my neighbor's truck
lets me sleep. Even the snail will get

a little help as it scales the oak branch
by our window on a short journey a light year
long and one hour faster tomorrow.

I Lived in Rags

I lived in rags beside the city wall
The days were dark and rainy
I drank the misery they handed me

ate the dirty food and drank their platitudes
swayed to the music and saluted.
All the while I kept one faith,

that sooner or later my troubles
would bore me. And that day came
wide as a field, long as rain

without a whisper or a warning
the wall collapsed on its own
and a harsh old kingdom was overthrown.

Lithium Days

One day you walk into a house you know well
and not at all, and enter the room where a breeze
whirrs from a rotating fan.

A blue jay peeks
in at a window and stares at you—a minute
like an hour. Traffic

beyond the trees
sends up a thin racket but it's fading.
The late sunlight pauses over a bowl

of pears, their rusty glow
coming back as you stand there.
My mother sleeps

on a velvet couch
in the middle of this room,
dreaming off the lithium

her face on her slender arm,
an earring glinting
in the late sun. Love and resentment

they are here together
like old relatives on a Sunday.
A pale silhouette hangs

on the wall
where a clock hung years ago
telling no time

in this new house
which is an old house where you
are always arriving and about to leave.

Walking with Joe

I dreamed I was walking with Joe Salerno
down a deserted road somewhere, maybe
it was in old Japan maybe it was because
there were distant snow-topped mountains
delicate as brush strokes on either side,
a wisp of trees bending in a wind we couldn't feel.
Here he was again that funny Zen spirit
long hair, a black leather jacket,
and wire-rim glasses, part professor
part biker, reciting poems,
joking about ambition though
he was plenty ambitious himself
—and somehow still was—talking about
his own obscurity with
a deep derisive laugh. A poet of tender
brilliance, gone so much too young, gone years ago.
But in this dream, after we had walked
For a while not saying much really
Joe noticed a man in a conical
straw hat had fallen in beside him
face hidden in hat-brim shadow, "Hey,"
Joe said with his old grin: "Isn't that Basho?
I think that's Basho."

Nothing for the Morning Paper

We have nothing for the paper.
The mayor isn't fucking the comptroller after all,
And the old senator near death is not dying
Not tonight. We have nothing.

This morning was so beautiful.
We had so much time., the words we would need
for the stories everyone dreamed of telling
were hauled joyfully like old graven idols to the newsroom:
Stunning, unprecedented, shocking, bizarre
Body in Trunk, homicide and war.

But there was no scandal today, no murder worth telling
And the same old wars. Just meetings, speeches
and press releases and the strike at the Ford plant
in its 51st day. How we'd love

to go back to the beautiful morning
and not fail like this. But now its deadline.

Acknowledgments

Atlanta Review: "Hat of the Moon";"Canoeing with Amy." "Pearls"

Carolina Quarterly: "Bankrupt Farm"

The Kean Review: 'Obit for Newsprint"

Lascaux Review: 'Sunrise Commute" (previously as "Traffic Jam Songs.")

The Missouri Review: "For Them."

The Mississippi Review: "Encouragement"

Narrative: "My Father Quoting Shakespeare Late at Night"

The New Guard Literary Review: "Somebody Wake the Verb"

NJ.Com: "Traveler's Song"

The New York Times: "Wasting the Day" (as "The K-Mart in West Orange")

Ploughshares: "The House of Old Age"

Southern Humanities Review: "Local Heroes" (as "Women of My Childhood")

Dogwood Poetry Journal: "Rain Dogs."

New Verse News: "Driving All Night in the Red States."

The Florida Review: Lost in My Own Garage

Big Citylit: Dear Beth

Troubadour: Red Peppers (contest honorable mention)

Oberlin: Daughter's Homework

"Gods of Vaudeville" appeared in *Tremble: The Vice Chancellor International Poetry Prize Anthology* (Canberra University Press, 2016)

"Local Heroes" was reprinted as a broadside (Newark Public Library, 2008). "and reprinted by *Silver Birch Press.*

"Love in the Kitchen" appeared in *Days When Nothing Happens,* a limited edition chapbook, winner of the Slapering Hol Press Chapbook Contest.

"Local Heroes" was featured on *Poetry Friday* on July 9, 2009.

These poems were supported by a Witter Bynner fellowship
From the Library of Congress, selected by Donald Hall

Acknowledgments

A beloved thank you to friends and mentors now gone who taught me and encouraged me, whose voices are still with us: Donald Hall, Robert Hayden, Philip Levine, Joe Salerno and Lemuel Johnson.

Thanks also to passionate journalists Amy Nutt, Suzanne Pavkovic, Mark Mueller and the incredible staff of the once great *Star-Ledger.* Truth Poets everyone.

And to Dr. Randy Mackin, professor, biographer, newspaper editor and savant of Southern literature, a veritable one-man band,

Thanks to the Hudson Valley Writers Center and its founder Margo Taft Stever, a engine of inspiration for poets.

Thanks to the Library of Congress for the Witter Bynner Fellowship which helped encourage this book